My life exposed

IT'S PAT!
MY LIFE EXPOSED

Compiled by
Julia Sweeney
and
Christine Zander

Photographs by Norman Ng

BROADWAY VIDEO

CADER BOOKS

HYPERION
NEW YORK

Chris Kunce courtesy of Dana Carvey

Models: Jennifer Aspinall, Steve Baumgartner, Albert Bechtold, James Biederman, Michael Cader, Mary D'Angelo, Ed Falco, Kamela Gallena-Jones, Meg Handler, Howard Handler, Stephen Hibbert, Charles Kreloff, Linda Lee, Erin Maroney, Norman Ng, Andrew Nutter, Mark Nutter, Laura Sigman, Toxic, Lesly Weiner, Tom Wicka, Christine Zander

Hair: Mary D'Angelo
Makeup: Jennifer Aspinall
Props: Danny Bleier
Costumes: Ed Falco
Production Coordinator: Lesly Weiner
Pat doll by Francesca Ingrassia and Debbie Pisaro
Pat logo by Bob Pook and Marlene Weisman
Art Director: Edie Baskin

For information address Hyperion, 114 Fifth Avenue, New York, New York 10011.

Cover and Book Design: Charles Kreloff
Additional Photos: Lesly Weiner
Produced by Cader Books

PHOTO CREDITS
p. 20: © Biophoto Associates/Photo Researchers; p. 38: © M. E. Warren, 1972/Photo Researchers; p. 40: Everett Collection; p. 41: © M. B. Duda 1989/Photo Researchers; p. 48: P. Giraudon/Art Resource; © 1991 Joel Gordon; © Archivi Alinari, 1989/Art Resource; p. 49: Museum of American Folk Art (2); p. 50: © David R. Frazier/Photo Researchers; p. 51: Bob Krueger—Rapho/Photo Researchers; p. 65: Madonna Inn; p. 75: AP/Wide World Photos; p. 83: Fritz Henke/Photo Researchers.

Library of Congress Cataloging-in-Publication Data

Sweeney, Julia.
    It's Pat!: my life exposed / Julia Sweeney and Christine Zander. — 1st ed.
        p.   cm.
    "Broadway Video."
    "Cader books."
    ISBN 1-56282-938-6 : $7.95 ($9.95 Can.)
    1. Saturday night live (Television program)   2. Pat (Fictitious character) 3.
American wit and humor.   I. Zander, Christine. II. Broadway Video, Inc.   III. Title.
PN1992.77.S273S94 1992   92-16081
813'.54—dc20   CIP

First Edition
10 9 8 7 6 5 4 3 2 1

Dedication

Julia and Christine would
like to dedicate this book to
Jim Emerson and Andrew Nutter.

Special Dedication

Christine and Julia received
very special help from
Stephen Hibbert and Mark Nutter.

Extra Special Dedication

Julia would like to especially dedicate
this book to two very important
Pats in her life:
her wonderful uncle, Pat Ivers,
and her lovely mother-in-law,
Pat Hibbert.
Two Pats who have nothing
whatsoever to do with Pat,
Pat Riley.

Contents

MASTER

SLAVE

Dear Purchaser:

THIS IS AN OUTRAGE!
WHAT YOU ARE READING IS STOLEN MATERIAL!

You see, for some time now, I have noticed that people are unusually curious about me. As far back as I can remember, people have asked me questions about myself. I wouldn't hesitate to even call some of them "obsessive." These people are strangely interested in me. And I don't know why! I'm just an average individual: I work at an office, I have a small circle of friends, and I live in a run-of-the-mill apartment. Their curiosity makes no sense!

However, recently, two women have been bothering me more than others. That's how I knew who to blame when my scrapbook turned up missing. These women are criminals!!!

I have contacted my attorneys and they are taking appropriate action.

WHAT YOU ARE ABOUT TO READ IS ILLEGAL!

Pat Riley

Pat Riley

Baby's Name Pat O'Neal Riley

Date of Birth October 13, 1961

Hospital St. Malachy's

Time of Birth 12:00 Noon

Baby's Weight 8 lbs. 2 oz.

Baby's Length 22 inches

Proud Parents Fran and Jean

Remembering the day

I will never forget the day Pat was born. I was making breakfast, and all of a sudden I felt the first contractions. We were so excited! We rushed to the hospital, and after a couple of hours, Pat was ready to be born. And I remember how happy I felt when the doctor shouted, "It's a baby!" I was so glad Pat was healthy, when we counted all ten fingers and toes. Pat was born with a full head of curly black hair. Just like Pat's namesake, cousin Pat.

Baby's first smile

2 months. When we tickled our new baby's chest, Pat would smile. We did that a lot! Kids are so much fun.

Baby's first sounds

Pat would only make one sound for the first year. Sort of a gurgle. I guess I would just spell it like this: eeeeuuwwww.

Baby's first tooth

8 months. Pat seemed to be teething forever!

Baby's special idiosyncrasies

Pat was such a drooly baby. Just constantly drooling! Boy, did we go through bibs.

Baby's favorite toy

A small little cow. Pat slept with that little cow for years! The funny thing was, when you turned the cow upside down, it went: "Moo!" But Pat's cow was broken, so it only went: "Ooooo!"

My favorite Toys

Halloween!
I love to pretend to be someone or something I'm not. Oh what a great holiday!

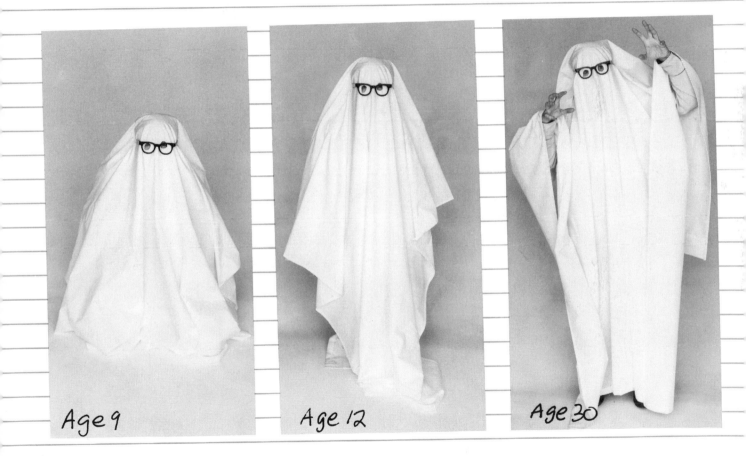

Age 9   Age 12   Age 30

The first time I was a ghost, it was a huge success! That's why I was a ghost on Halloween every year. I always say "Don't change what works." That's why I barely ever change my wardrobe. I have 7 baby blue western shirts, and 7 pairs of tan polyester pants.

My parents divorced when I was very young. But Dad moved next door and I split my time between their houses. My parents were overly concerned with the impact the divorce had on me. They felt that it was important that I get into some kind of therapy. I chose "Art Therapy." Here are some of my pictures.

ART THERAPY "Parental Divorce" Tuesday 4:30-5:30

Pat age 6½

Pat should continue art therapy for six months.
- Dr. Kreslow

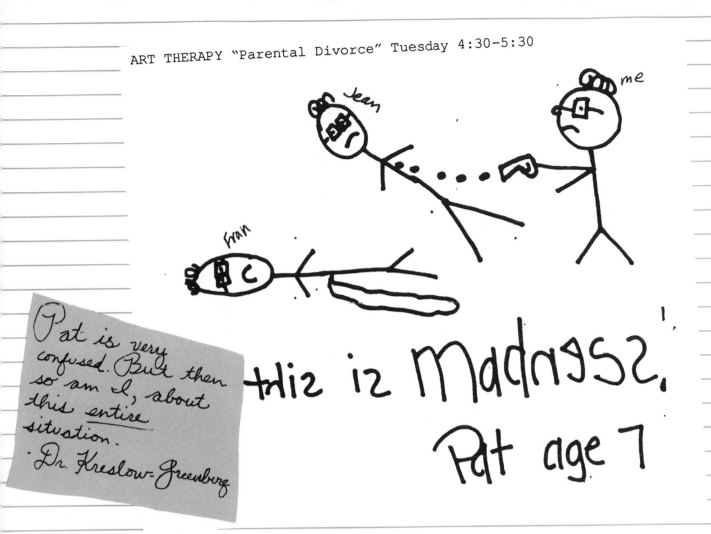

Pat is very confused. But then so am I, about this _entire_ situation.
- Dr. Kreslow-Greenburg

tHiz iz MadNeSZ!
Pat age 7

Neither of my parents remarried. (Even though Jean did run off with some idiot for a short time.) Right now, my parents get along better than they did when they were married. They claim it's because that they aren't trapped in role models that society forced on them. Now, they actually date each other! They're much happier living separately. Isn't life strange, sometimes?

Sometimes I feel so lucky that I'm a perfect combination of both my parents.

19

My Science Project

D+ Pat. This is very informative. But what do you think about this topic? How would we "humans" be different if we reproduced this way?

"ASEXUAL REPRODUCTION"
written essay
by Pat Riley
Grade 8

How would your life be different Pat?!? Please tell me!!

Mrs. Emerson

DEFINITION OF ASEXUAL REPRODUCTION:

In asexual reproduction, new individuals are produced by simple division of non-reproductive cells, from a parent system which germinate directly into a new individual. Asexual generations are essentially identical, because a single parent transmits its exact set of genes to each descendant, (like cloning).

ASEXUAL REPRODUCTION ADVANTAGES:

Asexual systems are prolific and quickly colonize new habitats.

Pat I have an encyclopedia, too! ! ! !

ASEXUAL REPRODUCTION DISADVANTAGES:

Organisms that are created as a result of asexual reproduction have a disadvantage over sexually reproduced organisms in that the latter can create variable attributes that can more easily adapt to changing environments.

THE MOST COMMON FORM OF ASEXUAL REPRODUCTION:

The most common form of asexual reproduction is called binary fission, in which the cell simply divides in two.

CONCLUSION:

In conclusion, asexual species do best in static surroundings.

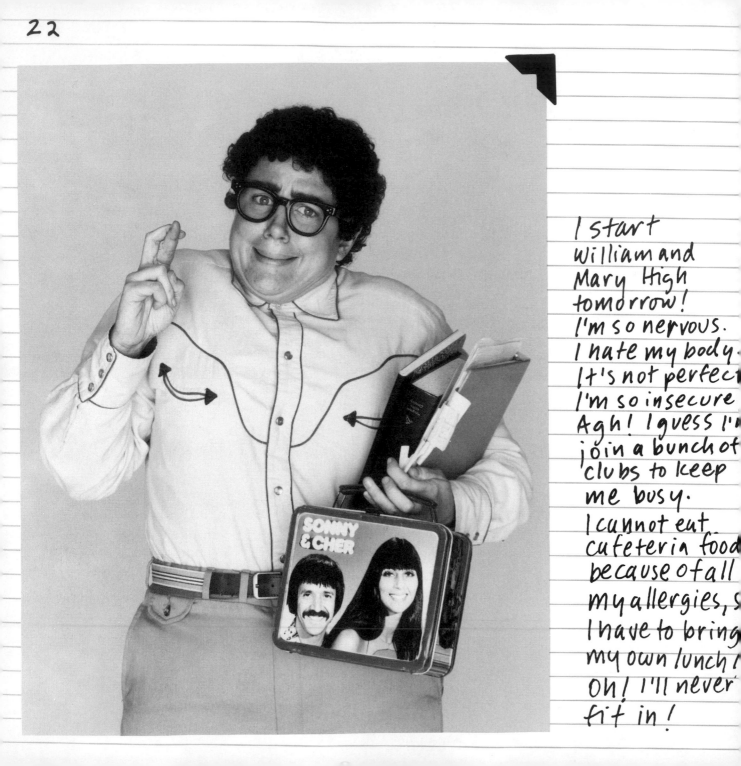

I start
William and
Mary High
tomorrow!
I'm so nervous.
I hate my body.
It's not perfect.
I'm so insecure
Agh! I guess I'
join a bunch of
clubs to keep
me busy.
I cannot eat
cafeteria food
because of all
my allergies, s
I have to bring
my own lunch
Oh! I'll never
fit in!

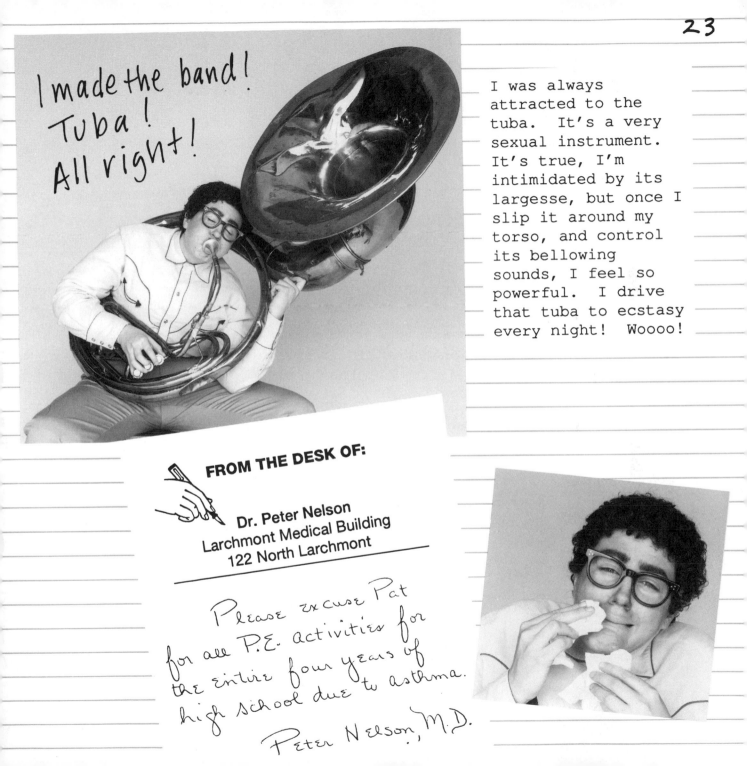

I made the band!
Tuba!
All right!

I was always
attracted to the
tuba. It's a very
sexual instrument.
It's true, I'm
intimidated by its
largesse, but once I
slip it around my
torso, and control
its bellowing
sounds, I feel so
powerful. I drive
that tuba to ecstasy
every night! Woooo!

FROM THE DESK OF:

Dr. Peter Nelson
Larchmont Medical Building
122 North Larchmont

Please excuse Pat
for all P.E. activities for
the entire four years of
high school due to asthma.

Peter Nelson, M.D.

Mrs. Pielli, *Dance Teacher*

The school forced me to take "American Social Dancing"

There's a difference in the numbers of girls and boys in the class. Mrs. Pielli is really upset. She keeps looking at me with a combination of confusion and hysteria.

Today, Mrs. Pielli screamed, "Don't stand around, just dance with someone! Anyone! A boy or a girl! All of you, just dance, damnit!" I guess Mrs. Pielli has decided that we aren't supposed to automatically take partners of the opposite sex. We're are all to learn to be leaders and followers and just dance with whoever is available.

How weird! Well, I'm just following orders.

RESPONSIBLE PROGRESSIVE PARENTS SOCIETY

November 3, 1976

William and Mary High School
1254 Tangera Lane
Los Angeles, CA 90036

Dear Staff and Students of William and Mary High,

We, the Responsible Progressive Parents Society, commend Mrs. Pielli on her open-minded approach to classroom dancing. Opposite sex dancing is definitely the more popular way to engage in dance, but we also appreciate that Mrs. Pielli understands that this is not the only combination. Society includes a large number of same-sex couples, and we are proud to include these people as Americans. Congratulations Mrs. Pielli, on your up-to-date attitudes! We are pleased to award Mrs. Pielli our highest honor, "Most Progressive Teacher of 1976!"

Sincerely,

John Epperson

Greg & Donna Higgins

Kevin Gunn & Charles Lane

Mike Shoemaker

Gertrude B. Toklas

Frannie Franken

Parents Group Riots Outside Classroom

December 12 (AP)—William and Mary High School was the scene today of a spirited protest by the organization, "Parents For A Brighter, More Traditional Tomorrow." The controversy surrounds a Ms. Pielli's "American Social Dancing" class and her decision to allow same-sex dancing amongst the students.

In an official statement Principal Vince Hanley announced, "Ms. Pielli has been an exemplary teacher here at William and Mary. However, to placate the parents we're immediately dismissing her and disbanding any and all dancing activities." Other classes were not disrupted by the protests.

Anyway I know how to dance the tango and the Foxtrot, both ways.

I hate you Pat Riley).
I hope the next time you
Bunny Hop you break both
your legs. Rot in Hell, you
little drooly creep!

Your unemployed ex-teacher,
M. Pielli

Ouch!
I found this weird
note taped to my
locker. I guess
Mrs. Pielli is
going off the
deep end.

joined the debate club.
hey are so cool.

SCHOOL YEAR 1976-1977.

DEBATE TOPIC:
"Survival of the Fittest, Fact or Myth?"

Only those serious about Debate should attend
the class.

NO GOOF OFFS!

SCHOOL YEAR 1977-1978.

DEBATE TOPIC
"Accepting people for who they are: Reverse
discrimination? or loving legislation?"

We will be voting on Debate Captain for the year
after school today.

The nominees are:

Pat Riley and Dana Murphy.

I lost! I guess I shouldn't
be surprised since
Dana has a remodeled
rec room and Mr. Murphy
works for coca-cola.

SCHOOL YEAR 1978-1979.

DEBATE TOPIC
"What is Pat?"

First meeting will be held Tuesday night in
Dana's rec room. Don't bother bringing soft
drinks. Dana's dad works for Coke!

Anyone welcome.

Oh very funny. I hate
Dana Murphy! Dana
is my nemesis!

Today I'm auditioning for
Puck in "A Midsummer Night's Dream."

I did some
research on the
character

This is a perfect
part for me

PUCK. In the folklore of England, Wales, and Ireland, Puck, also known as ROBIN GOODFELLOW, is a small hobgoblin who assists with household chores. Puck is also, however, addicted to practical jokes and is accused of responsiblity for the mishaps of domestic life. Puck's most famous literary personification is in Shakespeare's "A MIDSUMMER NIGHT'S DREAM" in which the dramatist merged classical myth with English rural lore to create an entire fairy kingdom in which Puck is the mischievous envoy of Prince Oberon and takes delight in the folly of human love. The adjective "puckish" aptly describes a whimsical delight in confusion.

PUDDING. A soft, mushy food usually made with a base of flour, cereal, etc.

PUFF BALL. A ... white-fleshed fun... touch when mat... brown powder.

PUFFIN. A r... a short neck, ... brightly colore...

PUG. A sm... a wrinkled ... curled tail.

PUGET'... cific, ext... Washing...

PURF... ration ... Coas... wour...

King Oberon: ....Clark Humphrey
Titania: ....Tiffany La Beau
Theseus the Duke of Athens: ...Richard Jameson
Queen Hippolyta: ....Debbie Cronin
Puck: ....Pat Riley
Bottom: ....Jamie Ivers

I got it! I got it!

The Stanislavsky Method

THE BASIC TENETS OF THE STANISLAVSKY METHOD INVOLVE FREEING SPONTANEOUS IMPULSES

I've got this down pat! No pun intended.

I have so much to learn! ➚

DIRECTIVE NOTES

PAT: LATE ENTRANCE IN SCENE 2
PICK UP YOUR CUES!
HANDS OUT OF POCKETS.
DON'T IMPROVISE! SHAKESPEARE DOESN'T
NEED YOUR HELP!

L O U D E R ! ! !

IF YOU NEED KLEENEX, BRING IT ON
STAGE WITH YOU.
DON'T UPSTAGE OBERON!

DON'T BREATHE SO LOUDLY. TRY NOT TO MAKE
SOUNDS INBETWEEN THE LINES.
GOOD PUCK LAUGH IN ACT 2.

REMEMBER — YOU'RE A NYMPH!
CLEAN YOUR GLASSES!!! WE CAN'T SEE
YOUR EYES.

PAT, YOU'RE PLAYING THIS AS IF YOU ARE
ATTRACTED TO BOTTOM — ARE YOU ???
OR ARE YOU ATTRACTED TO JAMIE?
IF SO, KEEP IT OUT OF MY PLAY!

OVERALL, PROMISING — CONCENTRATE —
YOU'RE ALMOST THERE.

Lyle D St. Aubin

← Feeling
Puckish!

WESTERN UNION

TO: PAT RILEY

FROM: MOM AND DAD

BREAK YOUR LEGS!   WE'RE WITH YOU!

WORK YOUR MAGIC!

Senior year! I get to play Pan!!!

The William & Mary H.S. Gazette

VOL. XXVII - No. X   "All the news fits!"   75¢

I'M FLYING TO SEE PETER PAN AGAIN!

Friday night was opening night of the William and Mary production of Peter Pan. Drama teacher Lyle D' St. Aubin directed this near-perfect Pan.

The surprise choice of Liliana Curtzman as Tinkerbell was topped by the bold casting of Pat Riley as Peter Pan. We all remember Pat's brilliant performance as the horse in Equus. But this young performer is full of surprises. Not particularly agile or articulate, Pat manages to spellbind us with an ambiguous chemistry. Versatile and cunning, Pat inhabits the character completely. Seeing Pat suspended in midair is at once frightening and exhilarating. We didn't expect such things from a neophyte! Pan is many things to many people, but Riley's Pan is for everyone.

D' St. Aubin says it was a joy to work with young Riley, "Pat always showed up in costume, and was in complete character for all rehearsals."

Also commendable is Dale Tazak as Hook. Musical arrangement by Ronald Skeetes is dreamy and hopeful.

—Al Rosenbloom

My Jobs

I'm babysitting at the Schreiners' twice a week now. Todd is so inquisitive.

Todd keeps asking me questions, like:

"How far away is the moon, Pat?"

"Pat, how many grains of sand are there on a beach?"

"Where do dogs go when they die, Pat?"

"Pat, are you a boy or a girl?"

I can answer some of these questions in an instant, but others would take a lifetime to explain. Babysitting is not easy.

↑ What a scamp!

They hired me at Chicken Doodles! My first job!

EMPLOYEE NAME:	Pat Riley					
HOURS	RATE	GROSS	FICA	FEDERAL	STATE	NET
14	$2.10	$29.40	$2.20	$8.35	$1.89	$16.96

I got fired today! The manager caught me stealing fries out of the fry bin while I was on duty. I guess I had grease stains on my chi and glasses.

6/21: Oh, well. I got another job! At Squeaky Clean Car Wash.

6/29: I learned Spanish from my co-workers. Did you know that in Spanish, every noun is either masculine or feminine? Talk about confusing!

7/10: The owner keeps pestering me, saying things like, "Hey, Pat, why don't you unbutton your overalls, it's mighty hot today!"

7/11: The owner announced that he's making the place a topless car wash! I quit on the spot. I do have standards!

"Today is the first day of the rest of your life."

JANIE PARKER
Cheerleader 2,3,4; Volleyball, 1,2;
Young Debutante Club 3,4: Queen of Gossip, 2,3,4

"Keep on Truckin"

MARK NUTTER
Football 1,2,3,4; Track 2,3; Big Penis brothers 3,4

"This is madness!"

PAT RILEY
Drama 3,4; Debate 1,2,3,4; Band 1,2,3,4; Archery 4;
Yearbook 3,4; Chess 1,2,3,4; Latin club 2,3

As you see I was very active in high School. That's because I'm such a people person.

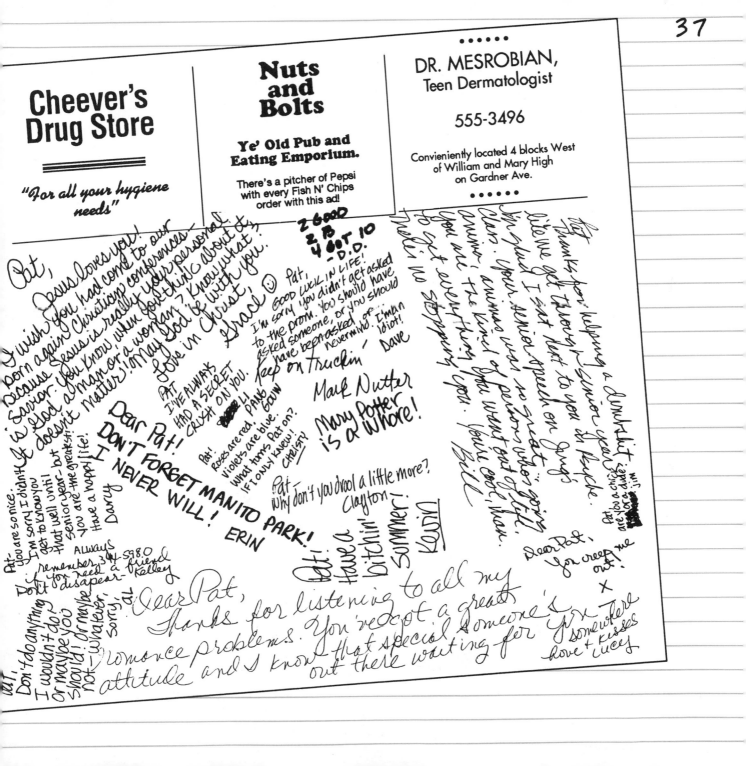

Pat,
Jesus loves you! I wish you had come to our porn again Christian conferences - because Jesus is really your personal Savior. You know, when you think about it, God doesn't matter! May God be with you. Love in Christ, Brad

2 GOOD
2 B
4 GOT 10
- D.D.

Pat, I'm sorry you didn't get asked to the prom. You should have asked someone, or you should have been asked or... nevermind. I'man idiot! Keep on Truckin' Dave

Pat, I'VE ALWAYS HAD A SECRET CRUSH ON YOU.

Pat! Roses are red, Violets are blue, What turns Pat on? IF I ONLY KNEW! CHRISTY

Mark Nutter

Mary Potter is a whore!

GOOD LUCK IN LIFE!

Dear Pat! DON'T FORGET MANITO PARK! I NEVER WILL! ERIN

Pat- Why don't you drool a little more? Clayton

Pat! Have a bitchin' Summer! KEVIN

Pat. You are so nice. I'm sorry I didn't get to know you that well until senior year - but You are the greatest! Have a happy life! Darcy

ALWAYS remember 344-5980 if you need a friend & disapear - Kelley

Pat, Don't do anything I wouldn't do? Or maybe you should! Or maybe not - whatever, sorry, Al

Dear Pat, Thanks for listening to all my romance problems. You've got a great attitude and I know that special someone's out there waiting for you somewhere love + Lucy

Dear Pat, You creep me out! X

Thanks for helping a dumb slut with... Pat, Thanks for helping a dumb slut... we've got through senior year like we got dealt to you & Psyche. & Psyche. & I sat next to you in Mr. plud your senior speech on drugs Clan. Your senior was no great anima; anima was a person who's going You are the kind of person who's still to get everything you want out of life. There's no stopping you. You're cool, man. You're cool, man. Bill

My Wild Year

My first year at college was a new beginning for me. You could say I "bloomed." I left old friends behind and became a very different Pat, a new Pat. I couldn't absorb the sights and sounds fast enough. It was a time of learning and a time of love. I started asking myself questions, questions like, "Who am I? What am I?" Questions that people had been asking me my whole life. I guess everyone reaches a point in their lives when they have to soul search. I did a lot of crazy things, but you have to remember, it was 1980.

I moved into a co-ed dorm in college. What an eye-opener!

GEORGE SAND HALL →

I love
my new
look.
←

That's me! →

Sharin' some thoughts and feelings in People's Park 1980! I'm questioning my sexuali

Everybody's experimenting! Right now I'm involved in a menage 'a trois. But this "two on one" is vaguely dissatisfying. I believe I'm truly only attracted to the opposite sex.

I went to a couple of EST seminars in Malibu. I got "It." As a matter of fact, I got "it" so well, that "it" became my nickname at the seminar!

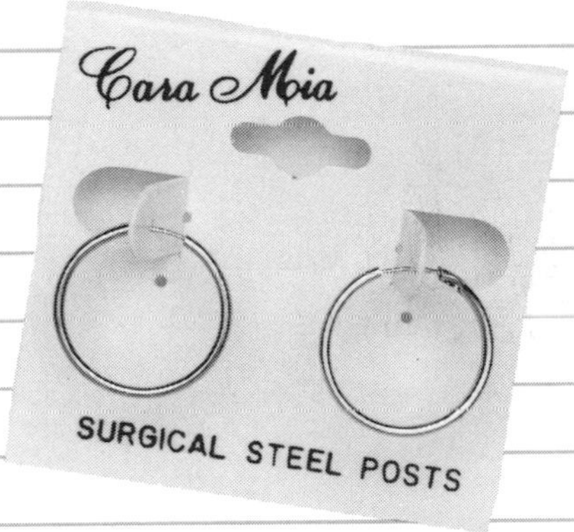

Cara Mia

SURGICAL STEEL POSTS

Should I get my ears pierced? Should I get one ear pierced? And which side? Doesn't the placement of a single earring give some indication of sexual preference? Forget it!

I saw a picture of myself with my "new look". I am such a weirdo! I must change my hair back — no one will ever take me seriously!

The Band

COOL WHIP
and Other Treats

I ran into three people playing
horns on the street in Santa
Monica. When they started
playing "Taste of Honey" I knew
these cats could swing! I had my
trumpet with me and I joined in.
We jammed all night! We decided
to form a band, and they elected
me as leader! We're going to be
the hottest Herb Alpert cover band
around! We papered the whole city
with our flyers.

We're getting a lot of
reservations, I guess the poster
is a little provocative.

PAT RILEY and the CAHUENGA BRASS
play your favorite Herb Alpert songs
Friday, 6 P.M.
at the Dresden Room in Los Feliz

43

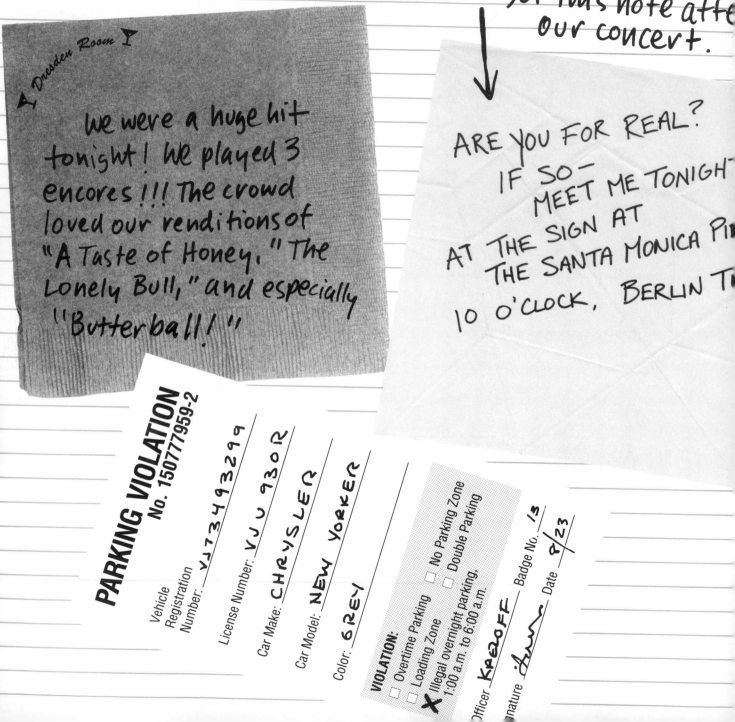

I got this note after our concert.

♦ Dresden Room ♦

We were a huge hit tonight! We played 3 encores!!! The crowd loved our renditions of "A Taste of Honey," "The Lonely Bull," and especially "Butterball!"

ARE YOU FOR REAL?
IF SO—
    MEET ME TONIGHT
AT THE SIGN AT
    THE SANTA MONICA PIER
10 O'CLOCK,   BERLIN TU

PARKING VIOLATION
No. 1507777959-2

Vehicle
Registration
Number: __VJ7349329q__

License Number: __VJU 930R__

Car Make: __CHRYSLER__

Car Model: __NEW YORKER__

Color: __GREY__

VIOLATION:
☐ Overtime Parking   ☐ No Parking Zone
☐ Loading Zone   ☐ Double Parking
☒ Illegal overnight parking,
   1:00 a.m. to 6:00 a.m.

Officer __KRZOFF__   Badge No. __13__

Signature __Anna__   Date __8/23__

asu turned out to be a very
nteresting person. A striking Asian-
merican with an exotic sense of play.
asu comes to our rehearsals now and
s helping us tremendously with our
usic selection and style. I trust
asu's ideas completely!

Kasu wants to sing. We've never
had a vocalist before. I think
the band will realize I'm right
when they read Kasu's lyrics to
"The Lonely Bull." Simply
brilliant.

♫ THERE'S A BULL
WHO WAS LONELY NOW,
OH SO LONELY NOW,
IS THIS BULL.
AND IT'S NO BULL ♪
THAT BULL IS ALL ALONE.
ALL ALONE HE WILL STAY. 𝄞

This is great!
Our band is
going to be
a huge hit!

Hey Tibs,
Kasu is ruining our band.
Kasu's a weirdo! What does Kasu
mean in Japanese? Tone Deaf?
If that thing opens its mouth
one more time, I'm walking!
— Crash

← I found this note stuffed in the bass drum of one of the band members

McGinty's Stag n' Mare Pub

STATEMENT

Profits to Band

Number of patrons in attendance: 3

Cover charge: $5.00

Percentage to band, 15% = $2.25

The band is in tatters!
They all got bent out
of shape when I
suggested Kasu get
the extra 25 cents. OK!
Nobody came! But I heard that
most of our posters were covered
up ~~by~~ with a lost cat flyer.
Fate takes its course!

The Music Seen!

Rumors of a rift in the Herb Alpert cover band, **Pat Riley & The Cahuenga Brass** are apparently true. The group has decided to call it a day. Inside sources tell us that the members are going their separate ways, after **Pat Riley** and unofficial fifth Cahuenga Brasser **Kasu** tried to change the artistic direction of the band. "We [Pat and Kasu] wanted more of a Trini Lopez sound." said Riley. ■■■■■■

Back to College!
I've got to
concentrate
on School!!
I'm getting
behind!

Things I Gotta Do Today!

① CHOOSE A MAJOR!

Philosophy

"To be is to do" - Sartre
"To do is to be" - Nietzsche
"Do be do be do" - Frank Sinatra

ANTHROPOLOGY - YES!
    I'm a people person!

Linguistics - Too much math

Physical Education - Asthma problems

Afro-American History - Too late.
                    Full, I tried.

Norse Mytholgy - No way, the
instructor is Mrs. Pielli. I don't
think you have to take partners
but I'm not taking any chances

Fashion Design - Too many weirdos

47

I chose Anthropology!
The study of people and how they evolved!

ANTH 210   M, W, F   8:00 a.m.   4 units

Our class went on a 14 day dig in Europe.
We were hunting for prehistoric fertility icons.

Christy Humphrey
found a classic
fertility goddess.

Bill Corcoran
unearthed a very
aroused satyr.

I found a Janus head!
My professor commended
me for my hard work.
She said I had the
brains of a Margaret
Mead and the insight
of Richard Leakey, all
wrapped into one.
What a compliment!

I'm taking an elective Art History course. We are
studying 18th Century American Folk Art. I am in love
with these paintings!

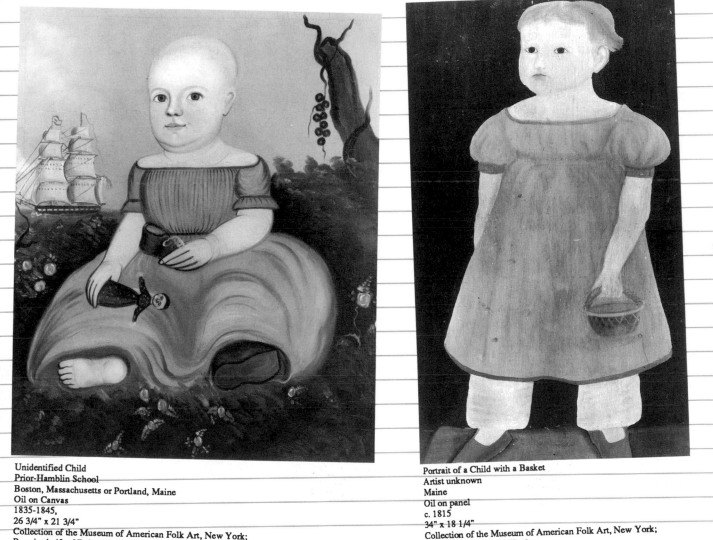

Unidentified Child
Prior-Hamblin School
Boston, Massachusetts or Portland, Maine
Oil on Canvas
1835-1845,
26 3/4" x 21 3/4"
Collection of the Museum of American Folk Art, New York;
Promised gift of Robert Bishop.
p78.101.1

Portrait of a Child with a Basket
Artist unknown
Maine
Oil on panel
c. 1815
34" x 18 1/4"
Collection of the Museum of American Folk Art, New York;
Gift of Mrs. Jacob M. Kaplan.
1977.13.1

Oh no! I must change my direction!

Anthropology isn't going to earn me the big bucks. I have expensive habits that need to be maintained. For example:

1. My western shirt collection
2. Fiesta ware
3. My fish tank collection
4. Marlene Dietrich photo collection
5. Calypso 45's collection
6. Salt and pepper shaker collection
7. Premium gas

I'm going to get a minor in Business!
I want to hedge my bets for possible jobs!

I did it!.
I graduated!

I went to the Ringling Brothers Circus in Paducah, Kentucky. I was strangely drawn to the bearded lady. We felt like we had known each other for years — bonding instantly. We were surprised at how much we had in common — our passion for Willa Cather, our interest in the supernatural. We've both felt like outcasts, me because of my overly keen insight into human nature, and her because of her beard.

I'm going to travel!
I want to see everything! What is the rest of
the country like? Are there people like
me out there?

T

BIG BUTTE & GORGE

M O N T A N A

ROADSIDE ATTRACTIONS

Bozeman, Montana

7 WONDERS OF THE WORLD

N A S H V I L L E

Oddity Museum
R E N O

MYSTERY CAVERNS

Arkansas

Ripley's
Believe It or Not
Museum
Chicago

My favorite places around the country!

I must enter the real world and get a job! Agh!

GLOBAL DOMINATION

PERSONAL DATA:

LAST NAME: Riley   FIRST: Pat

PRESENT ADDRESS: 124 Hencock Ave. #3-D Los Angeles

DATE OF BIRTH: I'm older than 18, and younger than 65.

HAVE YOU EVER BEEN CONVICTED OF A FELONY: Sometimes people say I look so it's a crime! (my little joke)

ARE YOU AFFECTED BY ANY PHYSICAL OR MENTAL CONDITION WHICH MAY AFFECT YOUR JOB PERFORMANCE: No, as long as I'm Surrounded by ragweed, moss or walnuts. And I'm not required to eat shellfish.

EMPLOYMENT DATA

NAME OF PREVIOUS EMPLOYER: Squeaky Clean Carwash

DATES FROM/TO: 8/78 - 5/79   YOUR TITLE: Final Rinse Simonizing Supervi

REASON FOR LEAVING: Management changed hands

NAME AND ADDRESS OF PREVIOUS EMPLOYER: Chicken Doodles Restaurant

DATES FROM/TO: 4/78 - 5/78

YOUR TITLE AND RESPONSIBILITIES: Beverage expediter and cup supply

REASON FOR LEAVING: Unsanitary Working Conditions

COMMENTS: I didn't work during my college years, because I wanted to dedicate myself fully to studying

EDUCATION: Cal State Dominguez Hills, B.A. in anthropology with a minor in Business Administration

EXTRA-CURRICULAR ACTIVITIES: (You may exclude any group which may tend to indicate your race, religion, national origin or sex) In that case I can't reveal any of them!

54

GLOBAL DOMINATION

Dear Employees of Global Domination,

Please welcome Pat Riley, our newest Clerk in Division Eight. We are very happy to accept Pat as part of our team. Please make our new addition feel at home and be ready to answer or ask any questions that might come up.

We feel we've never had the pleasure of having someone as unique as Pat. Pat's just one heck of a person. We think Pat will be a great asset to Global Domination.

Sincerely,

Morris Camp

Morris Camp,
V.P. of Human Recourses

Global Domination is an equal opportunit
We will not discriminate based on sex, race, or

ID # 062-45-328

GLOBAL DOMINATION
Pat Riley, Clerk
Division 8

There's Sue. She's so overbearing! I don't like that quality, in a woman! Or in anyone for that matter.

That's Bill. Bill is always kind of nervous around me. A nice guy though.

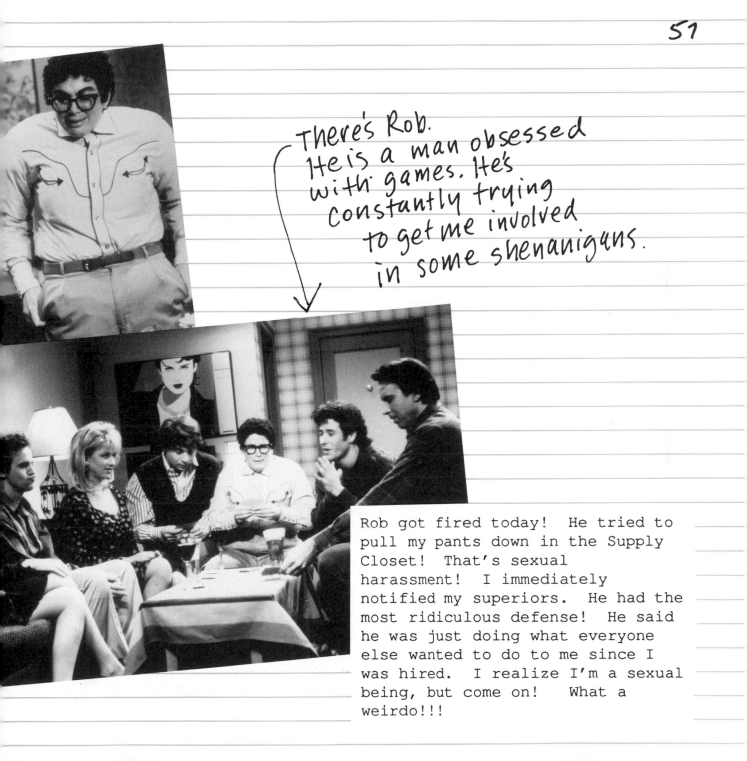

There's Rob. He is a man obsessed with games. He's constantly trying to get me involved in some shenanigans.

Rob got fired today! He tried to pull my pants down in the Supply Closet! That's sexual harassment! I immediately notified my superiors. He had the most ridiculous defense! He said he was just doing what everyone else wanted to do to me since I was hired. I realize I'm a sexual being, but come on! What a weirdo!!!

58

For Pat. R.

Date 1/31 **Time** 12:15

WHILE YOU WERE OUT

M Jamie Riley

From

Phone No. 555-1113

Area Code · Number · Extension

TELEPHONED		**URGENT**	
PLEASE CALL		WANTS TO SEE YOU	
WILL CALL AGAIN		CAME TO SEE YOU	
	RETURNED YOUR CALL		

Message I'm getting married to Trig. I want you in the wedding party! call me!

Operator

MY NAME IS PAT RILEY

X
_____ Will attend _____ Will not attend

Please reply by February 2, 1985

The wedding was a success. I met someone myself! Named Chris. My head was swimming! But, I was so engulfed in wedding party responsibilities, I had no time to flirt. I don't even know who caught the bouquet <u>or</u> the garter! Chris left me a phone number.

Should I call? Or should
Chris call me? Chris can find
out my number easily. Just
call Jamie. Oh I don't know what
to do - I'm too shy!

59

LEARNING HORIZONS
"THE PEOPLE SCHOOL"
PERSONAL GROWTH

CHOOSING THE RIGHT LOOK FOR YOU

Do you know what your "colors" are? How do you know that new fashion style is right for you? Should you dress down? Or up? Do you work for your clothes? Or do your clothes work for you? Should you accessorize?

Lolly Epstein, window dresser for two years at Sears & Roebuck has now agreed to offer this once in a lifetime workshop offer. You will learn all about fashion, its pitfalls and successes. Learn the difference between a sense of fashion, and a sense of style! Learn what "season" you are: fall or spring, earthtones or pastels. Learn to break out of tradition and be daring, without sacrificing class.

Lolly Epstein is a graduate of Lake County Community College.

Course fee: $29.00
Sec. A Feb. 11 5:30 - 7:30 p.m.
Sec. B Feb. 13 3:30 - 5:30 p.m.

EXOTIC DANCING

Do you know how to turn on your lover when you dance? Do you know the difference between being grotesque and being sexy? Have you always envied strippers? Why stand on the sidelines, when in four quick lessons you can arouse the best of them.

If you want to know, all you have to do is be willing, eager, ready, and sign up right now. Margaret Pielli, a trained dance instructor, takes you from belly dancing to lap dancing. Same sex partners welcome.

Margaret Pielli is a former high school instrtuctor and won The Responsible Progressive Parents Society award, "Most Progressive Teacher of 1976." She also happens to be an avid Norse Mythology enthusiast.

Course fee $89.00
Sec. K Mar 4,11,18,25 6-9 p.m.
Sec. L Apr. 9,16,23,30 7-10 p.m.
Sec. M May 7,14,21,28 8-11 p.m.

TALKING THROUGH TOUCH, THE ART OF MASSAGE

Do you like to touch yourself? Do you like to touch others? Do you know how to do it right? When your lover has a sore neck, do you know how to relieve the pain?

You will learn basic shiatsu, Swedish, and reflexology, all in forty-five minutes. Bring a spouse, or a friend, or just yourself!

Todd Skylar is a high school graduate from the Bay area, and is also a professional ski instructor.

Course fee: $19.00
Sec. F March 13 5:00 - 5:45 p.m.
Sec. G March 27 7:00 - 7:45 p.m.
Sec. H April 3 8:30 - 9:15 p.m.

ARE YOU A MAN OR A WOMAN?

Is your sexual identity clearly defined? Are people constantly asking you questions about your gender? Do you even know? Are you attracted to men or women?

Bingo! Is this the class for me or what?

I went to my first "Talking Through Touch" class. A miracle happened.

I was the first person in class, and as the others filed in I became anxious. Everyone seemed to have registered as couples, and I was all by myself! Then a few singles strayed in. But who would be my partner?

And then it happened. In rushed a wind-blown, out of breath, panting, Chris! Chris from Jamie's wedding! What an aura Chris has! Our eyes met. Talk about fireworks!

It turned out that Chris was the first of many late arrivals. But we knew. We knew it in our hearts. We were each other's partner in this oh-so-very sensual class, all about discovery.

We couldn't keep our hands off each other! In fact, the instructor, Todd Skylar, tried to force us to break up and work with other class members. Fortunately, our sexual chemistry was so powerful and obvious, no one would dare break us apart. We agreed to meet later for drinks. I'll admit it! We are in love!

FUNWORLD, USA

We were so amorous in the Tunnel of Love, that when we came out we were half undressed!

Chris got sick on the Giant Thrill Seeker 2000, a huge roller coaster, and we had to leave early. But we had fun anyway.

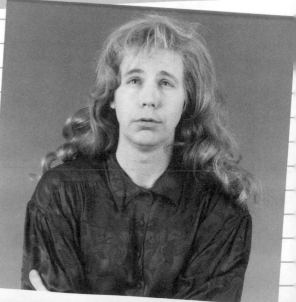

Valentine's Day, 1986.

Chris and I both sent each other a dozen roses! Isn't that funny? We think just alike!

Nuts & Bolts

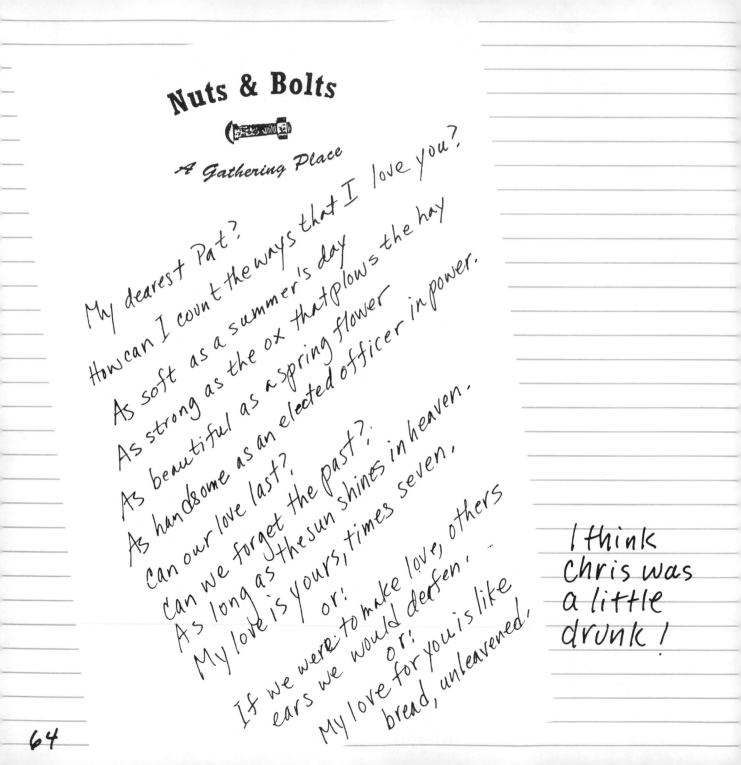

A Gathering Place

My dearest Pat?

How can I count the ways that I love you?
As soft as a summer's day
As strong as the ox that plows the hay
As beautiful as a spring flower
As handsome as an elected officer in power.

Can our love last?
Can we forget the past?
As long as the sun shines in heaven,
My love is yours, times seven,
or:
If we were to make love, others
ears we would deafen,
or:
My love for you is like
bread, unleavened,

I think Chris was a little drunk!

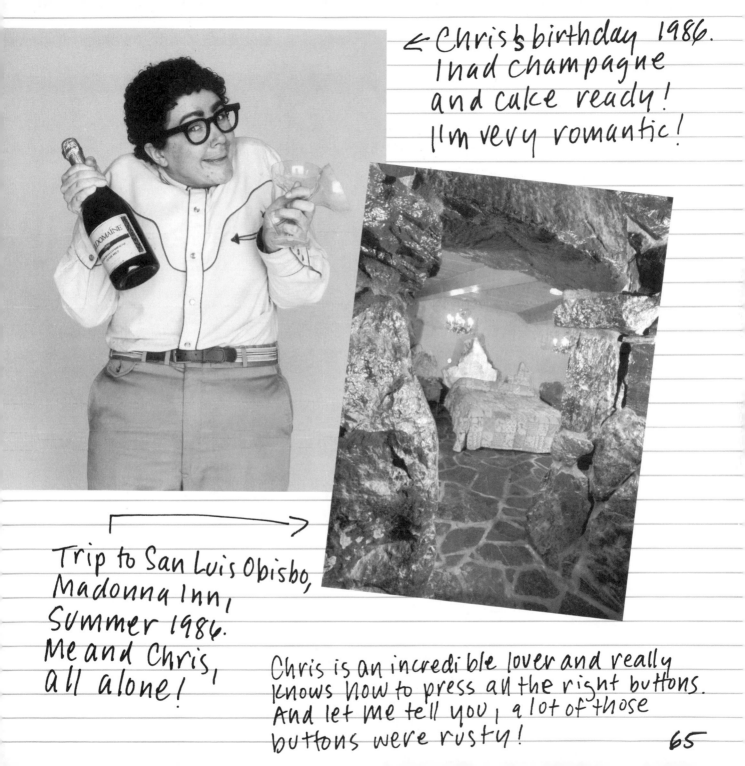

← Chris's birthday 1986. I had champagne and cake ready! I'm very romantic!

Trip to San Luis Obisbo, Madonna Inn, Summer 1986. Me and Chris, all alone!

Chris is an incredible lover and really knows how to press all the right buttons. And let me tell you, a lot of those buttons were rusty!

Gulp!
September 1986!
Chris and I move in together!

Chris' Chores:

1. Washing dishes
2. Laundry
3. Balance the checkbook
4. Recycling

Pat's Chores:

1. Cooking
2. Ironing
3. Spending money
   (my little joke)
4. Taking out the garbage.

Look what I found today! ↓

Hotel EARLE
"A DAY OR A LIFETIME"
Est. 1909

My dearest Terry,
How can I count the ways that
I love you?
As soft as a summer's day
As strong as the ox that plows
the hay
As beautiful as a spring flower
As handsome as an elected
officer in power
Can our love last?
Can we forget the past?
As long as the sun shines in
heaven,
My love is yours, times seven
Love,
Chris

My dearest Pat
How can I c...,
I love you
As soft a
As strong he ways that
the hay

As beau... ...'s day
As handsome as what plows
officer in pow's a spring
Can our love an elected
Can we forget?
As long a... past?
heaven...shines in
My, times seven
Love,
Chris

CHRIS IS
HAVING AN
AFFAIR!

There were problems. How did it start? Hard to tell.

There were little things that drove us crazy. For example, both Chris and I constantly fought over who should drive. We always opened doors for each other and it became confusing. And, I won't name names, but one of us kept leaving the toilet seat up and it drove the other one of us nuts!

And then there were big issues. Like, Chris didn't want children, and I did. Chris wanted to move to the country, and I didn't. I wanted to start our own business, and Chris liked working for "The Man."

Bigger than all of this, however, is the evidence that Chris has found someone else. My heart is broken.

The source of our misery

I'm so distressed after the loss
of Chris. I am so lonely! My
friend, Stuart Smalley suggested
I get a pet.

ay I found a stray cat outside
apartment. I took it in and
e it shelter.

I must get this cat fixed!
big problem: I can't figure
if it is a male or a female!
e just been guessing. I've
ed the cat Francy.

I'm embarrassed to even go to
vet - should I ask for spaying
neutering? And which procedure
s with which sex?

ended up just taking it to the
et anyway. I found out what sex
rancy was. Francy's new name is
rank. Looking back on it I
uestion whether I should have had
t done. Denying someone their
nnate sexuality is like playing
od. I'm not comfortable with
hat. But I guess it's for the
est.

Dr. JOHN M. DALY
Doctor of Veterinary Medicine

BILL

August 13, 1986
Spaying and Neutering

$40.00

OH DEAR! Today another
stray cat appeared on my doorstep.
Now I'm going through this all
over again!

71

I still have the acting bug!

If I don't try, I'll always wonder if I could I have been a star? I'm going to pursue this in my spare time, which I have a lot of, thanks to Chris. I find if I keep busy, I stay sane!

MONDAY, SEPTEMBER 28
ROSH HASHANAH

A NEW YEAR!
I will follow Jewish tradition and start my year anew!

TUESDAY, SEPTEMBER 29

Interview with potential agent, Tim - 2:30 PM!
(ask other actors if their agents have offices in their Mom's kitchens? But Tim does have an impressive array of clients' photos stuck on the fridge with magnets)

WEDNESDAY, SEPTEMBER 30

Audition - "Murder She Wrote" 3:15, for the role of THUG#2. Hmmm, I'm not too sure this is the kind of role I should be going out for...

THURSDAY, OCTOBER 1

Audition - "Designing Women" 10:40 AM, for the role as a guest at a bridal party! Boy, Tim's sure sending me out for a lot of different things, to say the least. I wonder what he's thinking?!

FRIDAY, OCTOBER 2

Audition - "Mr. Mom II" 11:30 AM, for the part of the guest at a bachelor party! That's it! I'm leaving Tim! He doesn't seem to get my "type" at all!!!

SATURDAY, OCTOBER 3

This acting business is too frustrating! The casting people smirked and derided the wonderful press clipping of my performance as Peter Pan I brought to the last audition with me! It's a wonder ANY talented people are working in Hollywood!

PAT RILEY

HT: 5'7"
WT: Variable
EYE & HAIR COLOR: Dark
AGE RANGE: 15-59

73

My favorite entertainer!
My favorite Song? "Leave Me Alone!"

Michael Jackson Performs Cosmetic Surgery on Chimp

Michael Jackson & Diana Ross, THE SAME PERSON?

MICHAEL AND LIZ TO WED, CHIMP TO PERFORM CEREMONY
Elephant Man Skeleton Is Best Man

DEC 13, 1986
Row C - 014

ARENA of the STARS
MICHAEL JACKSON
8:00 pm, December 13, 1986

14

Dear Michael,

I think you're great!   You are
one of my favorites!   One
question though, are you a man
or a woman?

Pat Riley

Pat Riley

Michael Jackson

Dear Sir or Madam,

Thank you for your kind note. Please continue to buy my records. Please encourage
your friends to buy my records.

Michael Jackson

P.S. Biologically, I am a man,
but I feel all of us have
feminine and masculine aspects
to our personality. However,
because of environment, culture and
even genetic make-up, we all have
tendencies one way or the other.

I have joined a Personal Interactive
Computer Service!   I can communicate
with people all over the world through
my modem!   What a wonderful invention!

I sent out this letter →

Dear Pen Pal,

My name is Pat Riley. I live in Los Angeles, California in the U.S.A. (Hollyweird!) My favorite color is grey. My hobbies are origami, cooking, bocce ball, fencing, darts, and playing the tuba!

I love music--all kinds, really. Some of my favorite songs are:

"Dude Looks Like a Lady"
"Both Sides Now"
"When a Man Loves a Woman"
"My Funny Valentine"
"There's a Place for Us"
"Lola"
"Leave Me Alone"
"My Way"
"A Secret Love"
"Is That All There Is?"
"Hey Look Me Over"

My favorite kind of "lazy day" is spent with a big bowl of Cheddar Cheese Popcorn and bunch of videos. I have a 35-inch TV screen! When it comes to televisions size really does count! (Grin 'n wink!) Some of my favorite videos are:

"A Man and a Woman"
"Victor/Victoria"
"I Was a Male War Bride"
"Pat and Mike"
"That Obscure Object of Desire"
"The Misfits"
"The Naked Truth"
"Some Like It Hot!"
"Tootsie"
"Repulsion"
"Ordinary People"
"Altered States"
"Guys and Dolls"
"Stop Making Sense"

My favorite TV show is "Unsolved Mysteries."
So please, Dear Pen Pal, write soon and tell me all about yourself.

Sincerely

Pat Riley

And I got responses from people all over the world. But these three pen pals are the ones I have the most in common with:

↳ Salehe Kitwana who lives in Zaire

what a cutie!

↳ Ulie Herzog from Germany

↑ Freedom Saunders from San Francisco, California

I collect restroom door art. Not the graffiti you find written by vandals on the inside of stalls, but the signs used to identify the women's or the men's bathroom. These are the most common symbols:

But I'm constantly finding these others that are a little less clear. Sometimes you can't tell which door to go into!

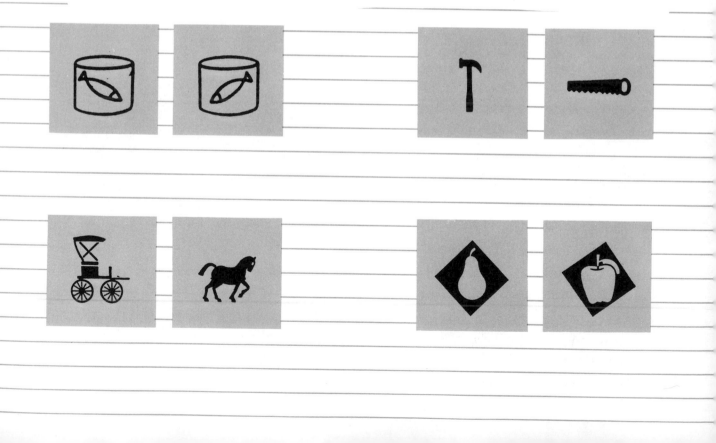

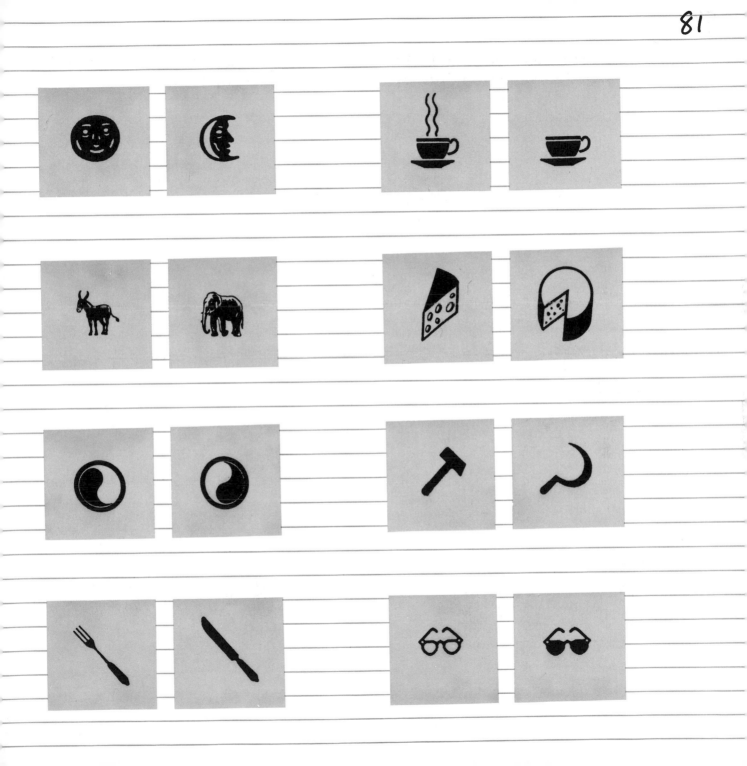

Trip to Jamaica 1988 /

This is my friend Roy, one of the fellas who worked at the hotel. I could tell he hadn't met many Americans by all the questions he asked me. But I eventually won him over.

←

Limbo,
Limbo!
Jamaica
is one
big party!

(Roy asked me to go to the nude
beach with him.   I WENT!!!!!   I
don't mind saying that I caused
quite a stir— probably because
I'm so well-endowed!)

Believe it or not, there's another person in my building named Pat Riley. Madness! He accidentally cashed a check to me that somehow ended up in his mailbox. It was a rebate check from the manufacturers of a blender I bought. It was for $12.50! I was outraged. I threw a huge stink. So he gave me a free basketball lesson.

I decided to keep a dream log on the suggestion of a friend who is a psychologist. I tried it for a month and wrote down my most significant dreams. Then I gave it up. What good does it do?

DREAM LOG

October 1

I dreamt I was a butterfly. I could feel the pollen between my legs. I straddled a telephone pole, and then flew into a tunnel. (What could this mean?)

DREAM LOG

October 10

I was in a war. First I was in the trenches, but the trenches weren't made with dirt, they were made with file folders! But I emerged victorious. I came out of the trench and built a very tall and narrow structure with the file folders. (This must have something to do with work!)

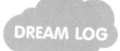

DREAM LOG

October 14

I started kissing Chris, and we started petting each other. But suddenly my parents came in the room and started hitting me. I had to protect Chris. But then Chris disappeared.

(These dreams are too Freudian!)

October 21

I dreamt I was riding on a bus and I had a baby with me. I guess that it was mine, and I felt like I loved it. The passengers on the bus kept asking me if the baby was a boy or a girl. I didn't know and I was embarrassed and when I would try to answer, no words would come out of my mouth. I hugged the baby to my chest, tighter and tighter, and when I looked down, it had turned into a piece of provolone cheese. (What does this mean? Maybe I should get into therapy.)

October 25

I was at work, getting some coffee at the kitchen area. Suddenly, I realized I was naked. But nobody noticed! I kept trying to cover myself up. I was embarrassed, and cold! Then, someone who was a combination of my boss and the Section 8 receptionist, started screaming, "Now we know! We were wrong!" I guess they could see me nude. I woke up in a sweat. (I'm not writing these dreams anymore, they're too emotional to recall!)

I don't want to spend money on therapy! Too expensive! I bought self-help books instead: "Eat to Win," "The Road Less Traveled," "What Color Is Your Parachute?" and "You Just Don't Understand: Women and Men in Conversation."

My collection of fortune cookie fortunes:

PEOPLE WILL LAUGH AT YOU

YOU ARE AT A CROSSROADS, CHOOSE WISELY.

MYSTERY IS THE SPICE OF LIFE.

YOU ARE ENIGMATIC.

NEVER FORGET YOU HAVE THE ABILITY TO BE ALL THINGS TO ALL PEOPLE.

DON'T ALLOW YOURSELF TO BE PIGEON-HOLED.

YOU ARE ABLE TO SEE BOTH SIDES OF ANY ISSUE

WHAT ARE YOU A MAN OR A WOMAN?

BYSTANDER SETS A SLIPPERY TRAP

Police photo: Victims approximate their positions prior to the entry of robber.

Larchmont Village was hit again last night by crime that has become rampant in the area. Cheever's Drugs, on the corner of Beverly and Larchmont, was the sight of an attempted robbery at approximately 7:05 p.m. Tippy O'Hara, the on-duty clerk, stated that the would-be robber entered the store threatening her with a gun, concealed in the pocket of the perpetrator's coat. Ms. O'Hara was waiting on a customer, Pat Riley, at the time. "I was helping a customer select a personal contraception item, and I was a little jittery because I wasn't sure what they wanted. And then it happened. The robber burst in and shouted, 'Give me all your money!' That's when (Pat) took over, it was great!"

It seems that Pat Riley became anxious and, when in a high-stress situation, suffers from an "over-salivation problem." Said hero began drooling heavily. The gunman moved toward the register with a crazed, doped-up look. Then it happened! He slipped in the pool of spittle generated by the frightened Riley. His head hit the candy racks and he was knocked unconscious.

"Pat saved my life!" the happy O'Hara shouted. Riley's only comment: "I tend to salivate when disturbed or aroused. I never thought it would save someone's life."

Store owner Howard Cheever is glad no one was hurt and is grateful Pat is a regular customer. When asked if he knew that Pat was made of the stuff of heroism, Cheever replied, "I never knew what Pat was made of, but I'm glad it saved Tippy."

My ethnic background is predominately Irish. But, I'm very proud to say that I'm also one quarter Native American. Along with our more traditional Irish family names like Pat, Kelly, Carol, and Lee, on the Native American side are relatives with lyrical names such as "Burly Dove" or "Brave Squaw" or "One Who Remains An Enigma." A brilliant people! So poetic.

THE GLOBAL DOMINATION INFORMER

"All the news that's permissible"

TALENT NIGHT'S A HIT!

Global Domination's Employee Talent Night was a smash hit! Watch out Cher and Robin Williams – these G.D. employees have talent aplenty!

Starting off the evening with an impeccable impression of Barbra "Prince of Tides" Streisand, was Andy Schell, assistant to Morris Camp. On a more serious note was Lisa Heath's emotional interpretative dance to the classic "MacArthur Park (Someone left a cake out in the rain.)"

But perhaps the most enlightening act was Section 8's own Pat Riley and protege "Lil' Pat." Maybe we've seen slicker ventriloquist acts. But we've never seen anyone with so much enthusiasm and commitment. We'll be looking for all you on "Star Search" real soon!

"NO REASON FOR ALARM," SAYS CEO

Regarding exposed asbestos in the employee cafeteria, CEO Robert "Bob" Cameron remarked, "The stuff's been there for decades! It's not like we're throwing it in the noodles!" Elaborating, Cameron commented, "This whole asbestos hysteria has really gotten out of control."

NUTTER TO HEAD TRUCKING

Graduate of William & Mary High and former star of the school's football team Mark Nutter has been named head of the Trucking Department. When asked about the promotion Nutter quipped, "Keep on truckin'!"

THINGS FOR THE COMING FINANCIAL YEAR LOOK GREAT, DESPITE RECESSION

"Things look great for the coming fir...

My ventriloquist act.

T: Good evening ladies and gentlemen! I'm Pat Riley!

LIL PAT: And I'm Lil' Pat!

AT: So, Lil' Pat what have you been up to lately?

LIL PAT: Oh, about two foot - two! **(Hold for laughs)**

AT: Very funny!

LIL PAT: That's my little joke! So, what is Pat short for?

PAT: Paaaaaaaaattt! That's my little joke! **(Hold for laughs)**

LIL PAT: Real funny. So, you're an accountant here, right?

PAT: Yes.

LIL PAT: Kind of a male dominated field isn't it?

PAT: Why do you think I got involved in it in the first place!

LIL PAT: Did you always want to be an accountant?

PAT: Yes...

LIL PAT: Ever since you were a little...? **(Hold for big laughs)**

PAT: Kid! Hey, Lil Pat do you have a boyfriend or a girlfriend?

LIL PAT: I'll have you know I only date puppets of the opposite sex!

PAT: I have such bad cramps!

LIL PAT: You do?!

PAT: Yes, I was on the StairMaster all morning, and my calves are killing me! **(Laughs)**

LIL PAT: Aw, Pat! You don't have to work out, I like you just the way you are!

Adrian and I met at the Washing Well laundromat. Our underwear got mixed up in the dryer! It was love at first sight!

Love is so mysterious... You never know where you'll find it!

It's funny, Adrian makes me think of the future. What will be? It's definitely time to stop thinking of the past, and to look ahead... who knows? Maybe we'll hear the patter of babies. A little Adrian? A little Pat? I'd like to see a tiny combination of both of us!

The Cahuenga Brass has gotten back together without me. I guess there are no hard feelings I've been replaced by someone named Cheryl Hardwick who wrote this song.

PAT'S THEME

I don't understand it, but it's a catchy tune.

[A] D   D sus.4   sus.2   D

A lot of people say, what's That? IT'S

D sus.4   sus.2   D   D sus.4   sus.2   D

PAT. A lot of people ask who's HE? OR

D7   **[B]** G   G#0

SHE? Don't Try To figure it out it'll make you cra-zy, in the

D/A   B+   B7   **[C]** Em7

sex-u-al AR-e-a it's kind of ha-zy. A Ma'am or a SiR, Ac-

F0   D/F#   B7

-cept him or her. for whatever it might be — IT'S

Em7   A7   D

Time for AN-Drog-e-ny — Here Comes PAT!

VR#2 transition   G/A   D   pno.

Dear Reader:

Well I hope you feel just awful! You've just read an illegal publication! If this sort of thing is allowed to continue, what other kinds of private material will be pilfered for public enjoyment? We must gather together as a people and make sure this sort of thing stops! Now you know every little detail about my life, and where has it gotten you? Nowhere! I guess you get to feel like a slimy little voyeur. THIS IS MADNESS!!!

However, I do feel compelled to answer one question. It's a question all sorts of people-- co-workers, strangers, and even friends--have been asking me all my life! It's difficult discussing it, but I feel that you, Dear Insistent Reader, know me so well now that I am compelled to bring it up. Besides, we all have our own "crosses to bear" and this is mine.

I am asked constantly if I'm a man or a woman! I can't understand it! To me and my closest friends, it is perfectly obvious. But that question is always there, haunting me!

So, to finally answer this matter once and for all, I Pat Riley, am a

Sincerely,

Pat Riley

Pat Riley

The end ?

PUBLISHER'S NOTE

The printer has informed us that, due
to circumstances beyond their control,
a few copies of It's Pat! may have
occasional smudges on assorted pages.

   We are very sorry about this situation,
and hope that it does not interfere
with your enjoyment of this rich and
rollicking account of Pat's colorful
life. Rest assured, we will make certain
that the problem is corrected in the
next printing.

CHECK OUT <u>WAYNE'S WORLD</u>: EXTREME CLOSE-UP

ANOTHER OFFICIAL <u>SATURDAY NIGHT LIVE</u> BOOK

AT BOOKSTORES EVERYWHERE
OR CALL 1-800-759-0190
Mon–Fri between 9–5 EST